PREFACE

An ode to all the wizardly wordsmiths
who preceded this inchoate iteration of me
and laid the facile foundations for
all the wondrous words I could weave

This, That & Life

December 05, 2015

my mattress, my sheet, my bed warm,
out of the way of imminent harm,
my office, my studio, my farm,
the allure of life, its charm!

my family, my friends, my best mate,
the healthy, hot food on my plate,
my racket, my ball, my skate,
so many people, things to celebrate!

my wish, my desire, my dream,
from rooftops, happy I should scream,
my brush, my color, my theme,
like a flan with a dollop of cream!

my thoughts, my lock, my key,
born to love, share, be free,
my I, my you, my we,
being the best me I could be!

Waiting While It Is

Sep 3, 2019

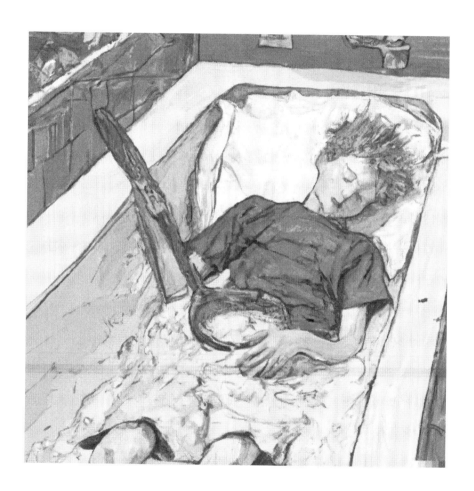

piece by piece i gather
those scattered moments
filling up my jar with dimes,
nickels and cents
i stow away the pain,
the ache, hide my tears
hoping in vain the dark
hungry rain cloud clears
for i have been fighting for us,
i have been strong
perhaps we've been waiting...
waiting for so long

sifting through the ashes
of our painted history
i don't know what i seek,
desperate to be free
to soar like an innocent
untainted white dove
trying to remember falling in
what they call love
i do not know who was right,
if i was wrong
but we have kept it waiting...
waiting for so long

emptying the space,
hidden nooks of my mind
i know not if anger, hurt
have made me blind
my instinct right now is
to swim, not drown
in the pool of misery,
to not let myself down
i missed the love story,
the romantic title song
haven't we been waiting...
waiting for so long?

gripped by fear, entering
a world of not knowing
i hope, i wish, i pray
that i will keep growing
for life does not give
everyone another chance
so i go on, smiling, coping,
living in this trance
fighting my demons, willing
myself to stay strong
knowing we have been waiting...
waiting for so long.

moving away, moving on,
flying away like a bird
no real honest truth
in any phrase, any word
for the heart bleeds,
leaving a piece of me behind
a friend, a mate, who is
caring, adorable, kind
i wish this would last,
that we weren't so wrong
but then we've both been
waiting... for so so long.

This Is Perhaps It

January 26, 2018

pacing up and down, dark thoughts i fight
waiting, desperate for her to come home,
willing the moon to shine brighter tonight,
texting, calling her unreachable phone,

looking at the hands in the clock,
picturing what might have kept her away,
hoping she's just around the next block,
saying all the god's names i pray,

twitching, eyes closed lying on my back,
aching for the end to this horrid dream,
planning my best course of payback,
choosing whether to shout, yell or scream,

straining to hear that evasive knock,
shuttling between anger and fear,
drowning out what the news people talk,
drinking coffee to keep my head clear,

trying to focus, breathing in and out,
reaching out to friends and more,
fighting my frail nerves, that doubt,
facing that dreading chill in my core,

cursing now, tired, helpless, cold,
hating every moment, eyes too dry,

feigning hope, lost at being bold,
berating myself, thoughts go awry,

struggling as i do, in she walks,
smiling, waving, blind to my sweat,
hurrying about, merrily she talks,
hale, under no kind of any threat,

breathing fine, no foul dramas,
joking that her silly phone died,
changing into her yellow pajamas,
unpacking her order of chicken fried,

stopping to see as i rise in anger,
raging, howling, bellowing steam,
serving the end of this cliff-hanger,
boxing my fist into the pillar beam,

claiming viciously her love lacks,
pulling away as she comes near,
slowing down finally in my tracks,
struggling to get my head clear,

fearing what she would make of this,
finding me in this strange land,
knowing how much i'd been to bits,

needing for her to hold my hand,

lowering my eyes i openly speak,
confessing openly my stupid love,
kissing her gently on the cheek,
loving hopelessly my angel dove,

pinching myself, saying a grace,
soaking in that smile, her wit,
thinking of my happy place,
concluding this is perhaps it!

Another Chance
Undated

a scarlet thought escaped my breath
got caught in the twine of a blue kite
that carried it beyond the grey clouds

floating free amid the cool creases
of those relaxed ripples of today
breathes a promise of another birth

when the sky caught fire
rising like a phoenix from my ashes
I decided to soar again

averse to the censuring gaze
not lonely or wistful, just being
the truest one can be

there beckons the new horizon
reminiscing the taste of a lost thrill
I start the journey once again

Unshackled

April 01, 2017

envying the tall boy at school
short, skinny, trying to act cool
amid taunts, no solace or relief
'it'll get better soon' his belief

staring at windows in the mall
awkward, alone, weirdly small
tugging at his sweater brown
hopelessness, a perennial frown

living in his own lonely box
spotted face after chicken pox
in pain, despair, air too thick
nothing but his shoes to kick

sprouting beard, dry and rough
doting parents not enough
to keep his welling anger at bay
life's bucket filled with dismay

holding that thought and this
grudging all that he did miss
while others made merry
sliding down that dingy quarry

trudging slowly, hiding, afraid
safe, sensible choices made

with honest prayers from the heart
some sweetness please with the tart
tasting joy, courting success but then
skeptical, counting if and when
he might lose the little he had found
what goes up might come around

rolling down the windows tonight
praying again with all his might
to set him free from this jail
just one happy passage in his tale

dreaming, tossing, turning last night
jolted, thinking "this isn't right"
for life is not meant for moping
"red's not my color", he was hoping

bristling leaves, dawn of the day
chirping birds flying to the bay
brought a smile, distant but alive
a will, a new promise to thrive

waking up after being awake
decisions, choices he must make
now, at this moment, today
like a mound of raw, wet clay

stepping towards the centerstage
unshackled, free from his cage
of misery, sorrow, sadness and fear
a brand new beginning so near...

Like Spoon & Knife

November 04, 2017

together, close, yet so far again
like tracks under a rusty train
amid the giggles, the joy tonight
brews an argument, another fight

partners, like spoon & knife
chosen companions for life
red roses, trips across nations
such empty, fake celebrations

practiced smiles, vacuous hugs
slime, murk gathering under rugs
walking together, hand in hand
over an unfamiliar, hostile land

the surf broken, the tide rough
finding love frustrating, tough
amid cavernous silences so stark
the air heavy, the sky dark

muddled thoughts, mayhem, chaos
that stifling suffocation of loss
trying to win a losing game
a hopeless moth to the flame

holding on, clinging for life dear
gripped by one ominous fear
eroding, shredding bit by bit
just a flicker where fires once lit

ironing the creases out in vain
aching in anguish, hurt and pain
tugging at shackles, pulling at chains
fighting to save a little of what remains

answer that question once more
closing with resolve that open door
what if to be whole, to be alright
means walking alone into the night

दायरा (The Boundary)

August 01, 2011

बिना शब्दों के गीत गुनगुनाता हूँ जो
उनकी धुन किसी को सुनाऊं कैसे?
खुली आँखों से जो देखे हैं सपने
उस मंज़र को यूँ ही भूल जाऊं कैसे?

एक राह पर अकेला चल पड़ा हूँ मैं
बेमाने रिश्तों में बँध जाऊं कैसे?
पीछे छूटे जो कभी चले थे साथ
खोने-पाने का हिसाब बताऊं कैसे?

कुछ आँखों में बस गया है जो पानी
चाह कर भी उसको सुखाऊं कैसे?
चटक कर टूटी चूड़ियों से बिखरे
सपनों के उन कतरों को उठाऊं कैसे?

वो लोग जिन्हे मैं समझूं अपना
बेगानों सी बात करें, ये सहूँ कैसे?
उम्मीदों की गूँज जो कानों पर पड़े
बिना कुछ कहे कुछ कहूँ कैसे?

कटी पतंग ज्यों उड़ती है हवा में
उस बेफिक्री उमंग से बहूं कैसे?
कल्पना की परिधि से परे
दायरों में बँध कर जियूं कैसे?

Chakra View

November 11, 2015

today i wake up, aspire, rise
relentless i toil, grow, flourish
u stand tall, prudent, wise
just passion, valor, no rubbish

i march, i conquer, i roar
no sleep, no fatigue or slumber
fierce, sharp, unburdened i soar
proud, royal, in a league asunder

unbridled, i fly like a knightly kite
chasing the path of celestial lights
cajoled by nothing, untamed, bright
a splash of color on cerebral whites

i am liked, followed, endorsed
reverence, admiration, applause
feels unnatural, fake, forced
the because of a lost cause?

wilting in the autumn sun
flustered, moaning, crying
no way out, no u-turn
desperate, decaying, dying

today i miss the mighty kite
rue the descent of the king

bemoan the curse of my sight
of the chakra, the circle, the ring!

Rest At Last

Undated

Hold on to drops of water
slipping through your fingers
Trust the random tide that
promises to carry you afar

Take a sharp u-turn down there
after the next curve on the road
Just there, here, yes anywhere,
now, let your shoulders unload

Where the dreams smile
and desires take flight
Afloat on that pillowy cloud
close your eyes and rest

The Future of A History

June 03, 2012

I still remember
the fine September day
when we first talked
shook hands, smiled
And the journey we took
over months and years
The endless moments of joy
new adventures, thrills
on the roads we took
and the corners we turned
together, hand in hand
A strange bond forged
in more ways than one
Our silences spoke
and thoughts echoed
Our being together
had no conditions
They said we were twins
fused into one soul
conjoined, entwined
blissful, happy
I saw myself every day
through your eyes
beaming with pride
to have you around
Glad to be cherished
being needed and loved

Yes, I had truly found
my person, my friend.
A decade flowed past
you nourished my soul
nurtured my belief
in being my true self
What goes up comes down
they say that about life
As winds of change blew
grew stronger every day
Out of sight really
became out of mind
You found new friends
new love, new companions
And as I look back
My vision gets blurred
Lost along the way
somewhere is my twin
My unheard silences
and muted thoughts
stay with me all day
desperate, in hope
As I go on, living
chasing my dreams
I still think of you
as my person, my chum
when in fact

I am quite unsure
of still being
your best friend...

Without The Within

October 24, 2009

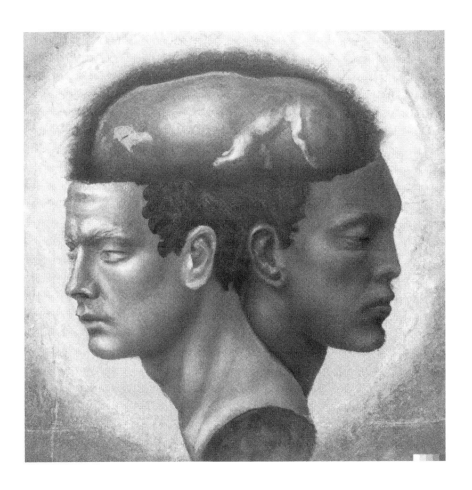

When a beggar spreads a hand
With calluses and a missing left toe
You wonder, debate and ponder
Pity welling, you frown your brow
A weak moment of ache
And a few cinereal coins go yonder...

When you hold the new National Geographic
And turn the unspoiled glossy pages
Emaciated kids stare from the center spread
Gnawing with misery of man-made cages
A welcome knock on the door
And you forget the tragic thread...

When waiting on a loved one
In a dreary, sterile hospital corridor
Amid septic fumes of anguish
Cries of agony, restless furor
A fresh corpse on the way out
And God receives a new wordless wish...

When fighting the fears of within
And combating the battles outside
In disparate arenas, with mismated ammunition
The two worlds overlap, invariably collide

A plain, somber introspection
And you discover the real villain within...

अंतहीन (The Endless)

July 17, 2011

गयी रात अपने मन में झाँक कर देखा मैंने
परछाईयाँ कई, धुन्दली धुन्दली सिमटी सी
दीवार पे लगे शीशे में अपने अक्स से लगा कहने
अंतहीन सन्नाटे में यादें कितनी बिखरी थीं

रात के तकिये पर, बनी सिसकी, बनी आहट
आँसू सूखे, खिड़की से बहती हवा, सहलाती थी
सिरहाने रखी तस्वीर, एक बस वोही थी राहत
बेचैनी, तन्हाई... आँखें खुली सोते भी

फिर मुलाकात हुई बिछड़े, दफ़न कर दिए जज़्बातों से
अकेली तन्हा रात में, यूँ खुद से बात करते ही
लॅब्ज़ भूलने लगे, काट रहे थे जो कपड़े पहने
मुझे भी कोई जाने, समझे, यही आरजू मेरी भी

एक रूहानी तपिश बुलाती, खींचती अपनी ओर फिर एक बार
साँसों की मद्धम आवाज़ बहकाती, सपने दिखाती सी
उठ जाऊँ, जागूं, ना मानूं अब इस अंधेरे से हार
ढूंढता अपनी पहचान था मैं कल भी, हूँ आज भी

The Erosion Paradigm
September 29, 2007

With the nascence of morning dew,
The arrogance of a thorn
While valley trekking, cooking stew,
Viewing humdrum with scorn
In the fleeting glow of fame,
The fake mirth, the borrowed name
Being embraced, my soul erodes...

Judging from the cover of a book
Saffron, soot, lilac, gray
Dust, silence in every which nook
Amidst ebullient walls, lonely I pray
Resplendent veneer, ash-laden inside
Question marks, without any guide
Lost in myself, my soul erodes...

Raiding the vistas my heart admires
Syllogistic reasoning almost divine
About the exuberance of wants, desires
Guides me, goads me out of confine
Fiscal friends, monetary mate,
Shun me, profess, critique, berate
Loving you, my soul erodes...

Watching the smoke rise in whorls
Around spaghetti straps, heels, wines
Wanton for innocent eyelash curls,

Simplicity for thou my heart pines
Cocktail lives, stirred not shaken
Quest for joy from a source mistaken
Watching you, my soul erodes...

In the crevices of my being
Shy, somber, yet hope floats
Like a buckram, I stand
Stiff, impertinent, my ego bloats
Like a mynah caught in a cage
With the stoic penance of a sage
Brooding alone, my soul erodes...

The Color of Hope
Undated

Swaying in the blissful blue breeze
Drooping under dainty dew drops
Dancing to bouncy bumbling beats
I sleep with my serene smiling self

Forgetting that bout of rebellious pain
Soaked in those pearly drops of rain
Standing away from bustling crowds
Under the happy tears from the clouds

Rising beyond the violet of a dying rainbow
Shedding the cracking camouflage of pretense
Deserting the stifling burden of a lame duality
Listen for those hushed footsteps of tomorrow

A Thought for Life

March 15, 2017

I live I think...

with empathy, never to hurt someone with intent
me true or false?

with passion, savoring the sweet and the tart
me better or worse?

with belief, doing nothing that I repent
me right or wrong?

with resolve, walking to the beats of my heart
me black or white?

with dignity, not living with my back bent
me weak or strong?

with desire, exploring realms on my travel
me pure or vile?

with joy, celebrating each tiny moment and event
me high or low?

with thrill, amid new stories, my words unravel
me happy or sad?

with thirst, seeking the next conquest

me first or last?

with vigor, just trying to be my very best

me alive or dead?

I think I live!

Fly High
Undated

standing alone away from the crowd
a spectre gently descends next to you
and entwines his fingers through yours

there goes your vanity away
a sliver of you leftover from yore
resplendent is your naïve flight

the uncounted crests beyond valleys
a savory aftertaste of that unbridled ride
ah...the heartbeat that just escaped

sands shifting under the feet
a heart riding the serene waves
burning with the colors of life

a few words too many
a familiar breath too close
another lifetime of becoming new

The Maze

April 22, 2017

the world of the living dead
the loop, the story, the hosts
the two minds within my head
the phantoms of morbid ghosts

the pull from beyond the precipice
the urge so strong, acrid, keen
the treasures hidden in every crevice
the desires yearning for the unseen

the empty kegs, the beer, the wine
the numbing melody in the air
the stained knife soaked in brine
the charade of this ghastly fair

the hustler swindling the swine
the hungry lusting for a kill
the bloody claim for what is mine
the reverie, the core of free will

the call, the whispers, the voice
the ringing of the chapel bell
the wrong but the right choice
the eternal damnation n hell

the pulp, the rind, the peel

the darkness darker than coal
the truest, the absolute feel
the death of an innocent soul

Imagine

Undated

When the rains seem dry
and the sun looks dull
When the stars appear faded
and the hug feels cold

Know that it's okay to cry
and to savor the lull
It's a moment to be traded
to break out of the mould

That perfect picture of us
you hold close to your heart
Is what drives the erring me
to unblemish me of my faults

That brooding stubborn question
unrelenting, dark, hidden,
Echoing loud once more
gliding under that white sunshine

A walk by the shore
waving goodbye to yesterdays
New adventures beckon
amid the shifting golden sands

Behold the wild blossom in the rain
the threshold of something new

On the fringes of sooty darkness

lies a lush bounty of imagination

ACKNOWLEDGEMENTS

Thanks to my family and my mates.
Gratitude for my mentors and my inspirations.
A big shout out to those whose lives I have heeded
to derive the emotions behind my words.

But most of all, I am grateful for the journey that my life has been.

I started walking this path alone, lost,
not knowing where it might lead,
I found some wandering words on my way,
and they morphed into verses...

A special mention to the photographers whose pictures I've used for the cover page (by HONG FENG), the one on the preface page (by Mathew Schwartz), and the one on the acknowledgments page (by Noah Silliman). And thanks to the creators of openAI (DALL-E V2) that was used to generate the amazing images for the title pages of the various poems in this book.

Made in the USA
Columbia, SC
12 May 2023

16530816R00030